CHOOSING HAPPINESS

AN UNCOMMON WAY TO FIND JOY IN YOUR LIFE

RÜDRANI DEVI

AC P

ACCESS CONSCIOUSNESS PUBLISHING

www.rudranidevi.com

Cover design by Remedy Creative / remedy-creative.com

Author photo by Karen Will Rogers / karenwillrogers.com

Choosing Happiness / Rüdrani Devi. – 1st ed.
Paperback ISBN 978-1-63493-276-9

This book is dedicated to my phenomenal friends,
Gary & Dr. Dain, co-founders of Access Consciousness®
I am so very grateful to have you both in my Universe.
How did I get so lucky?

What would it be like if you embodied so much consciousness in everything that you did, that others chose to become more conscious as a result of you? What if you were the inspiration for greater possibility? All it takes is for you to choose. YOU.

–GARY M. DOUGLAS

CONTENTS

FOREWORD

Let me be the first to congratulate you. For finding your way here, to this book, this conversation, and this amazing lady. This beautiful little book that you hold in your hands contains life-changing tools, conversations, and musings... some of which may seem so ridiculously simple that they couldn't possibly be valuable at all.

Guess again, my friend. The gifts, the insights, and the *choices* that Rudrani Devi so beautifully invites you to herein are some of the most profound I personally have found so far.

Happiness being a choice is a completely foreign concept in this world. Certainly happiness is simply a by-product of money, that perfect relationship, an easy life, or whatever else you have attributed it to. But what if we have it backward? What if all the things that you think will create happiness are actually by-products of the big, bold, different choice to be happy – *just because?*

This smacks in the face of American culture, and most of the world. We are all in pursuit of happiness, aren't we? Isn't it what everybody desires? If so, then why the heck are there so many unhappy people in the world?

The choice for happiness is a choice that sets you apart from the rest of the world. As Rudrani so courageously & intimately demonstrates in these pages, it's something that you can choose even in the most traumatic

and dramatic of circumstances. Rudrani Devi is walking, talking, smiling proof of that.

The choice for happiness requires us to let go of our
stories, of our fascination with being victim to the rest
of the world, and rise above all of it as empowered,
choice-ful people committed to creating something different in a world that is married to limitation.

While this may sound great and esoteric – the beauty
of this book is that it gives you pragmatic, applicable,
and incredibly easy-to-use tools to change your point
of view, re-direct your attention to what matters, and
become a rare being in the world who values, has access to, and chooses joy just for the sake of joy.

So get ready for a life changing read. Let these gems
soak in to your pores. Let Rudrani inspire the hell outta
you. Let go of everything you thought was real & true . . .
and step in . . . to you.

Enjoy, beautiful you.
And thank you for choosing.

Heather Nichols, MSW

Heather Nichols has been creating dynamic change in
people's lives for over 20 years. Her potent, spacious
presence invites you to say YES to the brilliant life that is
waiting for you on the other side of choice.

https://heathernichols.com

CHAPTER ONE:

BORN HAPPY?

Of all the people on this planet, why should I speak on the topic of happiness? Well, maybe because when people learn about my story, most responses I get are that I should probably be one of the least happy people, considering all that has transpired in my life. And yet, I consider myself to be one of the luckiest people I know. So, what's my secret? Hold tight and I'll get to that.

The way my mother tells it, I was practically scream-crying right out of the womb. I was that unhappy infant that if I wasn't getting attention 24/7, I would let everyone know. Loudly! There were nights where the only way my mother could sleep was if she was holding me in her arms. Right, what kind of real sleep would that be? You get the picture. Sorry, Celeste.

She loves to tell a story about when I was still a toddler and barefoot, because why would I want to wear shoes?

We were in the toy section of the Sears department store. I set my sights on a large stuffed lion that, at the time, was nearly four times my size. Evidently, I decided I had to have it, and cried and cried for days, until she went back to the store and bought the stuffed toy for me. I must have known something about that lion, as it became my bedmate, and the crying quietened. It didn't stop my insatiable appetite for life though.

I suppose it looks like I was a very demanding child, although the way I remember it, I just knew what I wanted and I would do anything to make it happen. I can only imagine the battles my mother had with my father to convince him that it was OK that I was interested in what ended up being many diverse adventures. Today, I would acknowledge that as being a true creator of my life. Whether an adventure proved generative for me or not didn't matter. I would just roll with it. I was inquisitive about everything; I learned a lot about a lot of things. From my point of view, I was driven. I wasn't angry, upset or unhappy. I simply knew what I wanted and at an early age, I would find a way, intuitively, to get it. I didn't give up or give in and I never quit.

About my life? I grew up under the heaviness of a very disciplinary Roman Catholic father who believed in the belt and would pull the sheets off the bed to wake up me and my five siblings every morning before school. He'd sing this annoying song, "Get up, get up, get up, get on your way. The sun will shine. You're feeling fine. Today's another day. No matter the weather, just pull yourself together. Ain't no use to cry, sigh, remember you're a lucky guy!" Ahhh, it was so awful even today remembering those seemingly positive lyrics, it still weighs heavy in my chest.

I remember my father backhanding me at the dinner table for saying the word "pregnant." My tooth split my lip but I wasn't allowed to cry about it. I had to go outside during a rain storm, and sit inside the metal shed with all the lawn tools and think about what I had done. I remember being cold, and deeply afraid that lighting could strike the shed and take me out. Sometimes I would pray for that. I remember pleading to God and saying, "Hey, I'd be OK with that. I'd be good in heaven. What about it?" My friends didn't want to come over to my house because they said my grandfather was always so angry. The difference in age between my mother and father was 17 years, so it was a common assumption that my father was my grandfather.

By the time I could drive a car, I was sneaking out and eventually ran away to my girlfriend Carol's house, because I decided I didn't want the harsh spankings anymore. I was very anemic, and I couldn't explain away the constant bruising. Carol's mother would call my mother and, crying, Celeste would come get me.

Forgive me as I take an uncomfortable pause as I reread my last words.

Thinking back on all that now, I still wasn't unhappy. Fear that my father might kill me one day would cross my mind occasionally, but I was made differently somehow. I did anything and everything I could to stay on his good side as much as possible. I signed up for student council, band, orchestra, the play house, the track team, dance classes and even mime classes. We also had a family paper route that was handed down from my oldest brother through all six of us, until my younger sister and I were in charge of it. With that came pet sitting when the subscribers on our route were out of town. I did anything I could to keep out of the house as much as possible.

In my earlier years, before I could drive, I found true joy in several things. There was a farm across the street from where I lived. I would play with tadpoles, bringing them home and keeping them in a fish tank until they grew legs and became frogs. I would pet the cows and I befriended the horse owners. I ended up being able to ride one horse they couldn't get to on a regular basis. I fell in love with a horse named Popcorn and swore he understood me. I found myself there nearly every day after school until my mother signed me up for dance lessons, and that time was then filled with dance classes. I had learned how to play violin beginning at age

four through the Suzuki method. With my mother being a classically trained pianist, I added piano lessons at
age seven. Eventually, as singing came naturally for me,
I decided I had to be in the church folk group, but as
they already had too many guitarists, I would need to
choose another instrument. I chose the banjo. I figured
they couldn't refuse me if I played an instrument that
no one else in the group played, and I was right! I was
the youngest in the group and occasionally was even
the featured vocalist.

I was also a tomboy and wanted to be an Olympic gym-
nast. I was very athletic and competitive with myself. I
could run a mile faster than any of the other girls in my
gym class. The paper route would have challenged any
adult due to the steep hills of my east Tennessee neigh-
borhood. In my gym class, I found that I had an affinity
for the uneven bars and the pommel horse. I begged
my mother, pleading for classes; but she couldn't find
gymnastic classes in such a small town, so I took ballet
and tap classes instead. Jazz and modern dance would
come a year later.

As it turned out, I loved dancing and discovered quickly that with classes right after school, I could be away
from home the majority of the day. Dancing and the
Playhouse entertained my whimsical side, and I could
be anyone. I liked talking a lot and still do! Evidently,
in my fathers' world, young children were meant to

be seen and not heard. I found out years later that his younger sister's children, were also terrified by him. Evidently, he took it upon himself to discipline them.

I found myself all over the place with band and orchestra classes, choir rehearsals, dance classes and eventually acting classes. I even signed up as the only girl rigger for The Oak Ridge PlayHouse's summer productions, eventually learning how to run the sound and work the spotlights. In these environments, with occasional friendly discipline from a firm but understanding adult, I was allowed to be my totally loud, expressive self. I was someone else when I was home. I was quiet there, but that kept me safe.

My senior year, with advanced placement prerequisites under my belt, I only went a half day for the last half of the year. I taught beginner piano, violin, and banjo instruction in the living room, while my mother taught piano in her studio. I got things done early because I wanted to be prepared for college, and so became a very young freshman at the University of Tennessee in 1981.

Whew, all of that by age 17.

It wasn't until college when I met other girls who were abused by their fathers and eventually, boyfriends, that I saw how different I was. From my point of view, they were either defiant and angry or shy and withdrawn. I, on the other hand, appeared to have a split personality. Out in the world, I was completely open and free to be who I was. At home, I became my father's child who craved his approval. It wasn't until I was really out in the world for the first time on my own, that I discovered I had this innate mistrust of the opposite sex. I took on the belief that if I was sweet, I would be safe. I would be sweet to all of them, cute or not-so-cute. Smart or whatever, you get it. I found that I wasn't really vulnerable with any man, which doesn't necessarily mean, I wasn't intimate. If I let myself get too close to any man, he might beat and berate me like my father did. I decided that in order to remain happy, I would need to remain free. I remember telling Celeste that I was never getting married, and became a chronic dater, disappearing when things got serious. That was young me, having and eating my cake, so to speak!

Is your head spinning yet? Are you thinking, "Poor delusional girl? So young and with her idiosyncratic beliefs. She must be mental!" Well, I'm definitely not normal. I learned that fairly quickly from comments like, "Why are you so happy all the time?" "Are you on drugs?" "What's wrong with you?"

What's right with me is where my head would go. I would answer those questions as the young, somewhat whimsical being that I was. "Ya know, happiness is just a choice. And it's what I am choosing." I never felt the urge to defend myself, as I could see that, like my father, the people that asked me these questions were not only skeptical, but deeply unhappy, glass-half-empty sad sacks. So I didn't waste my breath. They couldn't receive me unless I went down the rabbit hole with them. No other explanation was needed. Occasionally, I would just say, "Yeah, I'm crazy. Oh, well." And I moved on. I didn't care what anyone thought of my happy-go-lucky personality. My dad was the only one who could tweak me and so nearly until the day he died of colon cancer, exacerbated by diabetes and dementia, I found myself trying to impress him.

When I was 15, my father said, "You're beautiful now but not very smart. You better marry young." Well, I wasn't going to get married at all. I sincerely thought I had succeeded with that plan and then I found myself walking down the aisle two weeks before my fortieth birthday with a man eerily like my father.

CHAPTER TWO:

THE UNEXPECTED, PART ONE

Let's fast forward to November 2008. I was on what I considered to be a trip of a life time. I had been introduced to meditation nearly the minute I started college at UT Knoxville. After taking every religious studies course offered, I decided, I wanted to travel to India to see the ashrams and experience the culture. My wish was granted when Linda, a student, client, and dear friend of mine and of my clinic, gave me $4,000 towards a group adventure. It was a three-week excursion with an organization I had been with for nearly 23 years. Although the trip was going to interfere with Thanksgiving, Linda quickly decided she must go with me. After arranging for her to meet the meditation guru of Synchronicity Foundation in Virginia, she was approved for the trip, and we traveled together, even choosing to be roommates.

Here I was again, choosing what I wanted and being truly happy about it. So what if my marriage was rocky? At the time, so was Linda's and so together we were carefree gals, without a worry in the world. We would meditate, shop, eat and were enjoying all the new sights and sounds Mumbai had to offer. Our luggage was lost, so the first thing we did was go shopping, and we chose to buy typical Indian clothing. I alternated my fanciful outfits, even wrapping my head in a shawl, out of respect for the culture, with the jeans and T-shirt I showed up in. Fortunately, I could get laundry services every day, and the Oberoi Hotel had all the amenities covered. Linda got her luggage a couple of days later. Mine showed up four days before we were supposed to fly back.

Then the unexpected happened.

Have you ever had a moment in your life where everything changed and you knew your life was never going to be the same again? I've had two experiences like that. The first one was in college. The night before my first day of classes, I caught up with a friend who was a year older than me who suggested we hit all the fraternities as they were having parties to find potential rush candidates. We walked down fraternity row, stopping at all the houses that seemed interesting. There was one with a live band and PGA punch a-plenty. At the next one, people were playing beer pong and all kinds of drinking games. We must have had a rip-roaring time. The next morning, I woke up with a hand-written note practically on my face that said, "I tried to wake you, but you were out and I had to get to class."

Imagine the panic that set in and the massive headache that came with mixing alcohol, something I sincerely didn't know could happen. My Italian parents always had wine on the table and, although it might be mis-construed as bad parenting now, even when I was very young, they might pour me an inch of red. It was, after all, part of the meal. I had already missed my first class on the first day of college, and knew I had to get my act together. I grabbed my heals and ran barefoot from her apartment towards campus making the walk of shame into my dorm to quickly change, take aspirin, and hus-tle to admissions.

When I got there, I was informed that after missing class the first day, I would have to wait until the next semester to sign up for it. You see, there were always people on a waiting list for the core Communications classes, so if you missed roll call, there was somebody to take your place. Totally bummed out, I was told that all I would be able to take now was a choice of two elec-tives. Astronomy or Religious Studies. I choose the lat-ter and was then told that I would need to hustle as the class had already started.

When I got to the building and found the door marked with the room number I was looking for, I burst in and handed my paper to a seemingly startled, granola-looking guy.

"I'm a late sign-up." I handed him the paper.

"I see that," he replied. "Take a seat. I see one up there in the right-hand corner."

I looked to where he was pointing. This class had graduated seating, like a stadium, and all 200-something seats were taken. All but the one left-handed desk/chair combination on the very top tier. I made my way up the steps, past snickers, and did my best to hide my embarrassment. I sat in the desk that rocked to one side when I sat down and the teacher resumed teaching the class I had so rudely interrupted. He kicked off his Earth shoes, took off his round-wire rimmed glasses, and proceeded to sit cross-legged on the desk.

"So, there's really nothing for me to teach until we get into the reading," he began. "The first group of religions we're going to study will be Buddhist traditions. These are the pages you will need to have read before we meet again in class. So, let's do something fun. I'm going to lead you in a traditional guided meditation so you can get the feel for this culture."

Right then some jock looking dude stood up, pounded his fist on the desk and declared, "This is blasphemy! Jesus is my personal lord and savior!" And with that, he stormed out. Two others followed and after the upset settled down, the teacher quietly, in his very calm way said, "Good. This class isn't for everyone. Now we can begin."

I closed my eyes and as he spoke of a stream feeding into the ocean, I felt like I was going to a familiar place. My body seemed light and expanded, and I couldn't distinguish my arms from my legs, or my breath from the space around me. Then, I just blanked out. I was so tired from the night before, that for a split second I thought I was sleeping. Then, I sensed someone behind me and felt two hands cup my shoulders. The teacher was behind me and leaned in whispering gently, "I knew you were a natural when you walked in."

I opened my eyes. The room was completely empty.

Needless to say, I took every Religious Studies course offered as electives and ended up with a minor in Religious Studies. That's when I first considered that maybe there were many roads up the mountain, but the view from the top was the same. It seemed to me that every religion was searching and maybe it was just about the journey. It was then that I realized that I was taking the road to becoming fully me. My life changed forever in that moment and many adventures would follow.

CHAPTER 3:

THE UNEXPECTED, PART TWO

My life's journey eventually led me to that trip to India where I had my second life-changing moment. I chronicled the entire journey in my first book *Soul Survivor: a Healer's Pilgrimage and Homecoming*.

It was November 26, 2008, in Mumbai, India and Thanksgiving eve in the States. Our meditation group had been enjoying the day on a road trip to different ashrams and experiencing delicious traditional Indian cuisine. We were to have the next day off and I planned on doing some Christmas shopping for family and friends. Then, the last four days would be silent meditation and *darshan*, the opportunity to connect with local holy beings. We got back from our excursions rather late, so instead of journeying out to an Italian restaurant near the hotel we had been told was good, we decided to do our usual and eat in the Tiffin, a restaurant that opened into the lobby. The Oberoi was a four-star hotel, and we all marveled at the other patrons of the hotel who looked like royalty dressed in amazing *sattvas* and Indian-style *kurtas* adorned with intricate embroidery. There was a large group that we surmised must have been coming back from a traditional Indian wedding.

There were six of us at dinner that night, arriving much later than the rest of our group as most of them were already retiring to their rooms. We were three pairs of roommates, and we quickly settled into conversation about how fabulous our day had been. It wasn't long before we heard a popping noise and Michael, one of our fellow travelers, got up to see what the ruckus was about. He quickly returned and informed us that it was just local hooligans with firecrackers in the street, and that the staff said there was nothing to worry about.

Our food arrived, but before we could take the first bite, a surreal thunderous explosion of automatic gunfire interrupted our laughter. It got louder, and I quickly realized that it was inside the building, not the subtle pops we heard before. It was the loudest sound I had ever heard. My thoughts quickly registered that whoever this might be was more than likely interested in some diplomatic figure staying in the hotel; after all, this was a fancy hotel and we had seen the elegant clientele walking through the lobby with their entourages daily. "That must be what's happening," I thought.

I remember going into automatic pilot, telling my friends to get under the table and quickly playing dead. What seemed like an eternity, lasted maybe all of twenty minutes before I was dragged into the kitchen. Two of my friends were killed, shot execution style. We remaining four eventually managed to get out. The rest of the 40 patrons in the Tiffin were not so lucky. My right triceps had been shot out, and my neck was swollen from a bullet that had grazed my throat. The bullet that went into my right leg, shattered the bone and lay on my femoral artery. I felt myself leave my body several times. In fact, it was from that perspective, I later recalled and identified the two shooters to the FBI. They looked like children, wearing backpacks with a plethora of arsenal strapped to their tiny bodies. The siege went on from the evening of November 26th through the 29th. The 10 Lashkar-e-Tabiba Islamic terrorists would eventually kill 164 throughout Mumbai and wound another 308. All but one terrorist died. The sole surviving perpetrator, Ajmai Kasab, was captured before he could take the cyanide pill they had all been instructed to swallow to avoid being taken alive. He was later tried and sentenced to death. The media would later call this Pakistani terrorist attack, 26/11 or the Mumbai Massacre.

And so, my second most life changing moment happened with three bullets, and this time, everything really would change. My fragile marriage fell apart.

My deep friendships with my meditation community ended abruptly. I had to immediately close the doors of my clinic and embarked on the painstaking recovery that would consume more than two years of my life. I sold my three acres of lake property in Virginia, emptied both my IRAs and my entire life savings, and began selling off anything I could to keep from losing my home.

Yes, at the beginning of this book, I did say I considered myself one of the luckiest people I know, and definitely a glass-half-full type gal. I still do. As I chronicled in my second book, *For the Love of Running: a Marathoner's Journey from Victim to Victory*, it took running the Boston Marathon within four months of my recovery before I actually took a moment to look back at all that I had gone through. I lived in a wheelchair for half of my recovery, driving before I could walk again. Strangely, I found myself thanking the terrorists for getting me out of an exhausting situation with my partner at the clinic and my partner in marriage. I may have some bitchin' scars, both physically and mentally, but I got a do-over. I wasn't going to take my second chance for granted. This time my target would be to have fun and enjoy my life, which is what I had initially planned to do when I went to college. Full circle, I contemplated the times I felt the happiest. There were many. Even in my abusive childhood, I found joy in so many ways I never expected. Here I was in the middle of my life, wondering what

I could create from this point forward to keep me on track with my happiness target.

Then I remembered an energetic clearing statement I had been given by a chiropractic friend of mine. It was long and tedious, but it was designed to get me out of my logical head when I felt cloudy, and it always made me feel lighter. I found myself digging through my files, determined to find it. Sure enough, there it was with the title "The Clearing Statement." The organization was Access Consciousness®, so my next step was to surf the internet and see what I could find. With the Universe, in its perfect way, always supporting me, I was able to locate the organization and found a class in Franklin, only 30 minutes from my home. I went with the intention of simply taking the BARS® class, but quickly got sucked in and signed up for the 4-day Foundation® class that followed. I learned several tools that shifted everything for me, and I realized in that moment that energy was my first language. My practice changed dramatically, and with time, along with a lot of support from my mother, I was able to pay off all my medical debt and create a life I never knew existed.

Looking back now, I realize that those five days of classes also completely changed my life. That was 2012, the year after I ran the Boston Marathon. And with every year, I find myself happier and happier. How? you ask. I choose it! I chose for me first, and decided that if whatever I did, did not provide joy, then I would and could choose something different. And that, my friends is the premise of this book. What if happiness was just a choice? What if you could be happy simply by deciding that is what you truly desired? What if it really was that simple? Take it from me, I'm probably the least likely candidate to create so much joy from so much trauma, but then, like I said in the beginning, I'm different. Are you?

The tools of Access Consciousness® are how I navigated my journey to happiness, and now I'd like to share that with you.

The mantra of Access Consciousness® is "All of life comes to me with ease, joy and glory." I recite this 10 times every morning and every evening, and it certainly seems to have created my life in this manner. Co-founders, Gary Douglass and Dr. Dain Heer wanted to create our world as a more conscious place, so we could create change in ourselves and increase the possibility of changing the trauma, drama and insanities that are present in our lives. They knew that consciousness would be the possibility for this planet to eliminate all the created walls of separation. And so, it is my target, in the rest of my years on this planet, to embody so much consciousness in everything that I choose to do that perhaps others might choose the same. What if I could be the example and inspiration for greater possibilities;

after all, I was the source for creating the change I desired by choices I had made thus far. What could I create and generate now? It all begins with choice.

RÜDRANI DEVI

CHAPTER FOUR

WOULD AN INFINITE BEING TRULY CHOOSE THIS?

Choosing happiness sounds simple, but if it were that easy, wouldn't you, along with rest of the planet have already chosen it? I'm going to share with you 10 tools from Access® that I live by, and it is these tools that created the roadmap to my increasing happiness.

In all my spiritual journeying, I had many points of view that continuously changed. I had always followed the energy to create my life, even if it appeared to be leading me nowhere. If something felt light and my body felt excited, I went in that direction. If it felt heavy, the opposite was true for me. The outcome, even if it was months or years later, would reveal itself. Case in point, I represented a director that ended up being one of the executive producers and directors of the HBO series *The Sopranos*. Before the show aired, he sent me the pilot episode and there was one scene in particular that shook me. It was the scene where James Gandolfini's character Tony is in a bar having pasta with some of his crime family. He knows that a hit is about to take place. So, when the shooter enters the bar, we, as the audience, are on pins and needles until the moment Tony yells, "Get under the table!" His people drop to the ground and the unsuspecting target gets taken out.

That episode was particularly disturbing to me, and yet, is it a coincidence that my director friend happened to send me that episode? I didn't have HBO. Was it just a lucky break that I would respond in exactly that way when I was in a similar situation, saving my life and possibly three of the other five friends' lives under my table? I prefer to believe that it was the Universe's careful crafting, connecting Allen Coulter and I when I was a director's rep and our friendship continuing even after I stopped repping him, so that I would have the information I needed to stay alive.

I consider myself to be an infinite being, not just this puny body that animates itself in the world. If the Universe is infinite and all-knowing, doesn't it stand to reason that I, as an infinite being, am also all-knowing? How could I possibly be finite? Somehow, even though I wasn't cognizant of it at the time, I knew that my connection with Allen would someday give me the tools I would need to stay alive.

CHOOSING HAPPINESS

And so, the first tool I'd like to share with you is:

WOULD AN INFINITE BEING TRULY CHOOSE THIS?

This incredibly easy tool is super handy. Whenever I have to make any decisions, especially if they feel heavy and I'm stuck as to what to choose, I ask the question, "An infinite being would choose this for what reason?" If my choice isn't going to create and generate for me or others, why, as an infinite being, would I choose it? Choosing something that doesn't create becomes a solid, finite universe of limitation. Whereas, choosing as the infinite self that I am, even if it doesn't make sense on the surface, if I get that it will create more, then I'm in. I follow the energy of that.

Here's the best example of this in my personal life. I have on a few occasions, gifted a class to an individual, knowing they didn't have the funds, but that it would change their lives. They were ready to receive it. I only offer that when it feels light, which isn't often. Sometimes it isn't a kindness to gift someone when they are either not ready, or perhaps, not interested. In these circumstances, instead of feeling cheated, I ask the question, as an infinite being, "If I offer this, what will it create?" Could it possibly change their lives to the point where everything not only gets better for them, but for all those around them? Could they become so conscious from this class that they become an inspiration for others to want to create the same? Doesn't that create a more conscious planet when there are more conscious people on it? YES! No brainer! So, an infinite being would choose this because it creates and generates more consciousness not only in their world, but in the long run, mine as well. We share this planet, although most of us don't act like it.

Can you see how creating more consciousness would make me happy? It's actually kind of selfish on my part, but it's a win-win situation.

One student, turned friend, ended up trading services with me for energy sessions and Access® classes. This was a seemingly random gal I originally met at an aesthetician's office. I remember choosing this facility by following the energy. "Light" led me to this sweet being who was very skilled, a mother of two and very open to creating other possibilities for her and her family. It had been a struggle for her and her husband, and I sensed the frustration was very real for her. I had a few sessions with her, and eventually she came and took an Access BARS® class.

What's that, you ask? It's the first class offered in Access Consciousness®. In my experience as an energy practitioner, BARS® points works similarly to meridian points on an acupuncturist chart. There are these 32 points on your head which, when gently touched, effortlessly and easily release any thoughts, feelings and emotions that don't allow you to receive. These points contain all the ideas, beliefs and considerations that you have stored in any lifetime. For most first-time clients of a BARS® session, it's the first time they have allowed themselves to receive from another, other than maybe sexual intercourse.

NOTE: there is more explanation of Access Consciousness® and Access BARS® at the end of this book.

This friend and I traded for energy sessions and several of the Access® classes I taught. It was a mutual contributive exchange for both of us. One day, quite distraught, she expressed a new awareness she had that her husband had not been paying the house note for several months and that they were at risk of foreclosure. I immediately asked if it would be a contribution to facilitate some options for her and as it felt light, we had a conversation. Through a series of questions, measuring what was light or heavy in each case, our awareness was that it was too late to try and sell the property. Bankruptcy was the lightest choice, and although in the past I might have had an interesting point of view about that, because it was light, we studied that option.

Now, checking in with myself, I asked the question, "An infinite being would choose to get involved for what reason?" An infinite being has no agenda whatsoever. I had no agenda. My friend had chosen her circumstances on some level by choosing to not be aware of what was going on. But I could sense that she was at a place where she wanted to create something different. Granted, perhaps, in the middle of her shock and dismay, she didn't have all the tools that could help her navigate the most generative steps to take to get out of this predicament. But she did come to me and express her fear of what could happen next. So, I asked the question again, "An infinite being would choose getting involved for what reason?" Would an infinite being have a need to get involved? No.

But, what if I could create a different possibility for her and her family by contributing my time and awareness? And what if that changed the lives of all involved? Hers, her husband's and her children's? It felt extremely light, so I proceeded. No agenda. How was it going to help me out, save knowing that I contributed to a friend in need that was in a place for change, could receive it and take the actions required to change things in her universe? Who knows what else that could create for, not just their future, but for other lives they may touch by this experience?

A naysayer might say something like, "Have any of you reading these words known someone who was a perpetual victim?" No matter what you tried to do to help them, it seemed they didn't want answers and simply wanted to continue to identify as "the victim of cir-cumstances." Have you noticed that in some cases, they actually use their victimhood as a way to victimize and control you? It's as if their helplessness is their way of getting you to take care of them.

Well, that could have been true here as well; and if that had been the situation in this case, and it had felt heavy, I would have probably nodded and agreed that her life was in shambles and watched her and her family lose years of equity in their home. Does that make me an uncaring person? What if not placing significance on someone's choice was the kindest thing you could do? You may not align and agree with their decision. But can you be in allowance that they are choosing their outcome? More on allowance later.

In this 10 seconds, I sensed that she was ready for change. It read light the minute we started living in the question of what else was possible to change her situation. And so, I put together a GoFundMe page for my friend, and within 48 hours, they had the money to declare bank-ruptcy, and with that, they had time to put their home on the market. No lost equity and no more prioritizing meals over gasoline. The GoFundMe post on Facebook brought in others that wanted to help. Soon, complete strangers were donating Christmas gifts for her young children and gift certificates at local grocery stores.

Note that most selfless acts come from a place of no agenda. What if choosing to assist in a situation came from an innate sense of "What contribution can I be in this circumstance?" Perhaps those are the times that we step into our infinite capacities and give up the finite conclusions we have chosen as real and true. What if our world operated in that way instead of "What's in it for me?"

One of the most generative infinite beings I know of is Ellen DeGeneres. Maybe her name should be Ellen the Generous. She is always changing lives without any personal gain, save maybe the gratification of having the capacity to do so. She knows her involvement creates and generates for those that may not have the power to create it on their own. And that contribution shifts their reality into something that wasn't there before. Her mantra is "BE KIND TO ONE ANOTHER." You could say Ellen is a benevolent capitalist. In my interesting point of view, if we could all take a page from the Book of Ellen, our world would indeed be a kinder, gentler place.

Definition of *benevolent*: marked by or disposed to doing good
a *benevolent* donor

Definition of *capitalist*: a person who has capital especially invested in business (or in people)
industrial *capitalists*

Being in the space of "Would an Infinite Being truly choose this" is freeing and definitely a source of joy and happiness for me personally. It takes all the guess work out of any situation where you might feel stuck or feel as though you have no choice. So, my friends, I invite you to consider living in this question and see where it leads you. You might be surprised how freeing this one tool can be. But you won't know unless you choose it.

RÜDRANI DEVI

CHAPTER FIVE:

EVERYTHING IS JUST AN INTERESTING POINT OF VIEW

Here's a question I like that my mentor, Gary Douglass, throws out as a proverbial wedgie: "Do you want to learn to have freedom, or do you want to pretend that you want freedom?"

This question is being asked of the being who has decided they are the victim and have no way out. Interesting point of view, isn't it? And that leads us to the next tool towards finding JOY.

EVERYTHING IS JUST AN INTERESTING POINT OF VIEW

If you didn't have a point of view about anything in your life, what would your life be like? If you didn't place significance on how you think things should be or look like, what could that possibly create for you? What if we were more like our dogs and cats about our points of view? When a pet gets hurt, do you think they have a point of view about it? Really? But how many people do you know who continuously live from a moment in their life when they got hurt or sick, and identify with their point of view about what happened to the point that they can't seem to move beyond it?

I can relate. I remember when my husband left me two days after my knee surgery, because in his words, he didn't "ask for this." He was referring to me getting shot by terrorists and needing to be cared for. In his interesting point of view, that wasn't something he signed up for when we got married. In sickness and in health didn't include "my wife may never walk again." His closing line before he walked out the door was, "If you had died in India, I would have loved you forever." Interesting point of view, don't you think?

I did walk again and eventually got full use of my right leg. But, in the meantime, the interesting take-a-way I came to was that all men suck. Interesting point of view I had that point of view. As we know, not all men suck, but that was my point of view for quite a while on my journey to healing my body fully. I couldn't even look the opposite sex in the eyes. I assumed they all had the same propensity to leave when the going got tough. These feelings were exacerbated when shortly after leaving me, he impregnated his girlfriend and got married. He now has two children.

How did I get out of that no-choice reality of men suck? Well, in using the tool "Interesting point of view I have this point of view," I realized that my point of view was creating an opinion I could not seem to overcome. If I could get to the point of "no point of view," I knew I could create something greater. That "men suck" point of view was not going to contribute to me, and was, in fact, going to keep me stuck in judgement of not only men, but of myself should I decide to consider romantic relationships again. Can you sense how limiting that is? And, it couldn't possibly be true. Alter all, two of my favorite men in the world were such a contribution to me that the word "suck" couldn't possibly apply to them. I'm speaking of the two men I dedicated this book to, Gary M. Douglass and Dr. Dain Heer. They co-created Access Consciousness® and these tools I'm sharing with you in this book that got me back to my true nature of being a happy being again.

"Interesting point of view I have this point of view" is about knowing what's true for you. It gets you to the place where you don't have to buy into anybody's reality. Just because it's their point of view does not make it real or true for you. Feel me? Why would you want to make something in someone else's world significant in your world? And if you choose to not make anything significant in your world, only perceiving it as an interesting point of view, imagine the freedom you could feel? What if you could just say, "Interesting point of view they have that point of view?" Something that works for them may not be something that works for you. That's a pretty easy assessment. If it's light, maybe it is something to consider. If it's heavy, it's a no-brainer, move on. We make things in our lives important so we can judge them and, with that, we can dismiss them. Did I really want to spend the rest of my life dismissing the male population? No. That definitely wasn't working for me.

And now, let me share a part two to this tool. In Access Consciousness®, it's called "The Clearing Statement," and for a full definition, you can go to:
www.theclearingstatement.com

A little back story of how I discovered the clearing statement. I was in a partnership with a chiropractor in 2003 wherein we sold high-end vitamins. One day he told me that he had discovered a magical statement that could unwind anything I might be feeling stuck about. It sounded strange to me at the time, that I could just ask something to change in my life and then after saying or reading this long clearing statement, voila, magically it would clear. I thought, "What group of crazies has he fallen into?" But I wrote it down. Although it was kind of clunky and long-winded, I could sense a shift every time I used it.

I ended up filing away the long-winded statement and after time, forgot about it. It wasn't until after my marriage had officially ended, I had run the Boston Marathon and written two books, that I remembered that strange, long-winded magical statement that could shift things just by me saying it. Where was that? Fortunately, I am that person that saves things I think I might be able to use someday, and after about twenty minutes of searching, there it was. It was two pages long and still didn't make any sense to me, but I could feel my body relax as I read over the words. At the top of my college rule paper, I had written the words "Access Consciousness." It was now 2012, and we had Google, so I researched and found that the clearing statement had been greatly abbreviated. It still didn't make sense, but again I could feel a shift of energy when I said it. My logical, problem-solving mind hadn't been able to achieve clarity about most anything in my life, so again, I followed the energy, creating and generating the changes I had been seemingly looking for, even if I couldn't quite put my finger on it.

I eventually understood that the clearing statement was designed to bypass the logical, thinking mind and would bring up stuck energies that had been keeping me unconscious. The purpose of the question was to bring up as much of the energy of limitation and judgment as possible about whatever point of view I might have that I wanted to clear and then blast it out of existence with the clearing statement. And, I didn't even have to say it out loud.

So, let me share that dynamic magical statement with you so you can try it out for yourself. It goes like this:

Right and Wrong, Good and Bad, POD and POC, All 9, Shorts, Boys and Beyonds®

Again, you have the website for more information.

Putting the clearing statement together with the tool, "interesting point of view" can very quickly, not only get you out of judgement, but also to a place of true freedom and happiness. Let me share further how I was able to get out of my judgmental, limiting "Men Suck!" point of view.

Interesting point of view I have the point of view that all men suck. Everything that is, and everything that brings up for me, I am now willing to destroy and uncreate it all, times a Godzillion. Right and Wrong, Good and Bad, POD and POC, All 9, shorts, Boys and Beyonds®.

CHOOSING HAPPINESS

I put this statement on a loop, and played it on silent every night for several days, and suddenly I noticed my personality had changed. I became more comfortable in my skin and more openly flirty. It wasn't like a switch was flipped overnight, but I was noticing men, and I liked it. And, oddly, I was noticing me more. Without all these points of view getting in the way, I was free to begin truly living my life again. Anytime anything got me stuck, I went immediately to "interesting point of view I have that point of view." Or if someone else's point of view got my panties in a wad, I would go to "interesting point of view they have that point of view." Or even better, "interesting point of view I have that point of view about their point of view."

You see, the clearing statement along with interesting point of view suggests this as a different way of perceiving, knowing, receiving and being in your life. What if there was no right or wrong, no good or bad? What if everything was just an interesting point of view?

So, I invite you to consider living in "interesting point of view" for the next few days, maybe even creating some clearing statements around the things that are not working in your life, and see if you can perceive a shift. Or not. It's just a choice that could set you free.

RÜDRANI DEVI

CHAPTER SIX

LIVE IN 10 SECOND INCREMENTS

This reality is so funny to me, no wonder I'm laughing all the time. It's like, God gave us all the one thing we don't desire and that's FREE WILL, which in my understanding is the ability to choose anything whether it makes sense to anyone else or not. It brings me back to the earlier question posed to me when I was so much younger and allowed myself more free will. "Why are you so freakin' happy?" And I would say, "Because I choose to be." It made more sense than choosing not to be happy. It didn't matter that no one else got it. It didn't matter some people had the point of view that I must be delusional or on drugs to be this free in my expression of exuberance. Oh, well, I suppose in their interesting point of view, they didn't really have free will to choose something different.

That's where the next tool I'm going to share with you comes in. Some may call this, living in the proverbial now. Access Consciousness® calls it:

LIVING IN 10-SECOND INCREMENTS

What if you realized that you can choose things other people choose not to choose? Like Happiness? Maybe, in their interesting point of view, they don't have the capacity or the right to choose because of their responsibilities or their religion, so they don't choose. It's almost like they are waiting to deserve it to choose it. How do you create a life if you surmise you can't choose for one reason or another? Interesting choice to not choose something different. Interesting point of view they have that point of view.

What if living in 10-second increments put you in the energy and space of always creating your life? Something doesn't work in this 10 seconds for you, you can always choose again, and again, and again until it does work for you. And then, maybe in a week, it stops working for you, but guess what? You have the free will to choose again. How cool is that?

Instead, what I see is people living from their projections and expectations, destroying the possibilities they could be choosing if they were living in 10-second increments.

For years, I had a very interesting point of view that I wasn't talented enough, or that I didn't possess the capacities or capabilities to facilitate more than a 1-day energy class. I would tell people, "I love to teach, but those long workshops aren't for me." Instead I hosted workshop after workshop of 4-day Foundation® classes, surprised by how much of what the facilitator was talking about, I already knew. It took one of my dear Access Consciousness® friends that had taken nearly every class I had either taught or hosted to say to me, "When are you going to teach this Foundation® class?"

"Not for me!" I rebelled again, and yet, she quietly persisted. "What would it take to create and generate that?"

Why wasn't I choosing it? Did it really feel heavy in those 10-seconds? Not really, so, why the resistance? "All the points of view I have surrounding what it would take for me to teach the Foundation class, I destroy and uncreate it all, times a Godzillion. Right and Wrong, Good and Bad, POD and POC, All 9, Shorts, Boys and Beyonds®."

Something started moving. I pondered longer, and as I was driving to Paducah to teach another Access BARS®, 1-day workshop and two body-processes—another 1-day workshop—I contemplated for a few 10-second increments, "What would it take if I choose this?" Another tool in Access Consciousness® is "What would my life be like in 5 years if I choose to do this?" If it was light for me, regardless of what it created, I would go that direction. I used this statement in dating, and although it hasn't created "the one" relationship, there have been many coffee or cocktail meet ups in which, maybe there was no chemistry, but there was something experienced. I always walk away with something I wouldn't have gained had I not gone on the date.

And so, there I was driving to Paducah, living in the question every 10-seconds. "What would it take for me to create this? What would my life be like in five years if I choose to be an Access Certified Facilitator®? You see, if I choose to became a CF, not only could I facilitate the 4-day Access Consciousness® Foundation workshop, but also a myriad of other classes that could be fun to facilitate."

Then I got the awareness to text Gary directly, "What would it take for me to be in Costa Rica in 10 days for the Certified Facilitator's training?"

I didn't expect his seemingly immediate answer of "don't stop asking the question."

I didn't. I had an hour to get to Paducah in time to teach the mediation class that evening. Traffic had been slow in some spots, adding 90 minutes to my drive time, and there I was, a stream of constant statements. I took living in 10-second increments to a whole new level. Choosing to live in the question, made me so light that as I cleared more and more every 10 seconds, perceiving the idea of being a CF and teaching longer workshops, I became joyful of the idea of choosing it, perceiving it and being it! How does it get any better?

I arrived just in time to facilitate the meditation class, and the next morning shared my desire to choose to be more than just a 1-day facilitator for Access Consciousness®. There were four in the class that said they would be interested in me coming to Paducah and teaching the Foundation® class and that they would pay upfront to get me there. The certified facilitator's training in Costa Rica was a financial commitment that, after all was said and done, along with prerequisites, would cost me nearly $10,000. Would four students cover that? No. But in those 10 seconds and the several following it, it felt super light. And every time I asked what my life would be like if I chose it, it was like my head was blowing clean off my shoulders.

So, in those 10 seconds I chose it.

The cool part about the Universe is that it wants to gift you. It's not about deserving it. Do you deserve to breathe the air? It's there for everyone, with no judgement of who deserves to breathe it in. Hidden deep in the Bible, there is this phrase I like quite a lot: "Ask and it is given." No statement has ever been more true for me, provided I don't go into the judgements of whether I can create it or not, or deserve it or not. It's just about asking. Once I put it out there, it was like the Universe was falling all over itself to create and generate what I was asking for. The cool part was that it never showed up like I thought it would.

Case in point, I was required to have $5,800 paid up front before I arrived in Costa Rica for the intensive, week-long facilitator's training. Normally, I would have been collecting money in a wish fund for a payout that large, but in this case, I just chose it, and so the creating began. I had only collected $2100 from my encouraging future students, so every 10 seconds, I asked what else was possible. The first thing that showed up was a no-interest for 10 months credit card after paying the initial 1.99% upfront. For $110.20 upfront, was this how the Universe was going to help me create this class?

This reminded me about the drowning man story where a fellow was stuck on his rooftop during a flood and asked God to help him.

He prayed to God for help. Soon a man in a rowboat came by and shouted to the man on the roof, "Jump in, I can save you."

The stranded fellow shouted back, "No, it's OK, I'm praying to God and he is going to save me."

So the rowboat went on.

Then a motorboat came by. The fellow in the motorboat shouted, "Jump in, I can save you."

To this the stranded man said, "No thanks, I'm praying to God and he is going to save me. I have faith."

So the motorboat went on.

Then a helicopter came by and the pilot shouted down, "Grab this rope and I will lift you to safety."

To this the stranded man again replied, "No thanks, I'm praying to God and he is going to save me. I have faith." So the helicopter reluctantly flew away.

Soon the water rose above the rooftop and the man drowned and went to Heaven. He finally got his chance to discuss this whole situation with God, at which point he exclaimed, "I had faith in you but you didn't save me, you let me drown. I don't understand why!"

To this God replied, "I sent you a rowboat and a motor-boat and a helicopter, what more did you expect?"

So I asked myself in those 10 seconds, "Is that how the Universe is going to help me create this class? What else is possible now?"

I decided to check out my balances on Venmo and PayPal, and there it was. I hadn't used PayPal credit since I bought my bio-mat for my holistic healthcare practice, and there it was, $5,000 at my disposal, for zero interest if I paid it off in 6 months. In the next 10 seconds I asked again "What else is possible now? What would it take for PayPal credit to allow me to borrow the entire amount?"

I filled out the credit request and it was granted in seconds. Ask and you shall receive. You just can't have a judgement about how it's going to show up.

Living in 10-second increments, you will always be creating your life. Expectation and projections of how it has to show up will always stop your creation or destroy the creations you could be making. It was just a choice to choose in those 10 seconds, and the 10 seconds after that, and the 10 seconds after that, and look what it created?

In the month that followed my CF training, I taught three Access BARS® classes, facilitated an Access BARS® trade for my students and taught my first 4-day Foundation® class in Paducah, Kentucky. It was more than enough to pay for the CF class. The funny part was that two of the original four students that said they would pre-pay for the class backed out, and magically two others I hadn't foreseen taking the class, signed up and took it. If I had a point of view about how this was supposed to show up, would I have been able to live in the 10-second increments that got me there? In the past, if my judgements of how that should look, be like or show-up for me, hadn't worked, my answer would have been no. If I had stayed in my expectation and projection of how I thought this should be created, I wouldn't have been in the space of creating it as the Universe perceived I could receive it. How cool is that?

Gary and Dr. Dain explain it this way: If you have 10 seconds to choose the rest of your life, why would you choose what's right or what's wrong. Why wouldn't you look for what's possible? Why would you try to figure out what makes somebody else happy?

If I only had 10 seconds to choose the rest of my life, I know what I would choose. I did it when I felt myself leaving my body in Mumbai, India. I remember my fleeting thoughts of I'm dying. There are two people that this will be very tough for. My mother and my husband. As it turned out, not so much for the husband. But the realization I had was, I'm OK with this. I'm a happy person and it's OK that this is it. What else is possible now?

And bam, I was back in my body. It never shows up like you think it will, folks, so stop fantasizing about how you can receive. Just choose and what you desire will show up for you. And I don't mean fake choosing. I mean, decide in every pore of your body. God knows when you are for real, even when you don't. Word.

CHAPTER SEVEN:

LIVE AS THE QUESTION

So, what if every answer or conclusion you ever came up with was a way to stop you from having awareness of anything else? Have you ever had a friend that decided after a date or two that this guy was "the one" and with that conclusion, could not see anything else beyond the answer to their dreams? Never mind if he's unemployed, or unkind or married. Yes, I'm being extreme, but you get the gist, right? It's the same way with anything. You decided that the answer to your happiness is going to be that white picket fence, the 2.5 cars and 3.5 children. Never mind that none of that even makes sense.

What if instead of living as the answer, we lived in the question? A very simple tool in Access®, and a question I ask when I don't even know what question to ask is, *what else is possible*? It's a great place to start when you find yourself stuck. There have been many inspired inventors and creators before us that have asked this very question. They see the way something is being done and decide that it's just not enough. Or it could be done with more efficiency. Or perhaps they see something that could be created that has never existed in this reality before they asked. They were willing to search out and see what others were not. They were inspired to ask what else is possible that I'm not seeing here? Remember, ask and it is given. You have the free will to ask. These pioneers might fail at their first twenty attempts, but they continued to ask. Remember the Wright Brothers, Orville and Wilbur? They were two engineers and inventors that wouldn't stop after each failed attempt to fly a plane, It wasn't until December 17, 1903, four miles south of Kitty Hawk, North Carolina, that they made the first controlled sustained flight of powered, heavier-than-air aircraft. Although they were not the first to build an experimental aircraft, they were the first to invent aircraft controls that made fixed-wing powered flight possible. They were willing to say, "Well this didn't work." And instead of giving up, they continued to ask, what else is possible now?

When you decide it can't be done, you solidify the possibilities and your fixed point of view becomes a finite, no-choice, stuck-in-the-mud reality. Whereas, should you be so bold as to live in the question of what is possible now, you open the door and invite the Universe to show you the infinite possibilities. As I mentioned before, The Universe really does what to gift you. That was so true for me when I chose to do the CF training. I followed every light choice which presented other possibilities for me to choose from. And each light choice led me to ask again and again and again. How fabulous is it that you can ask again and again in every ten seconds?

And so the next tool I'd like to share with you that has been a very large source of my journey back to authentic happiness is:

LIVE AS THE QUESTION (NOT AS THE ANSWER)

Gary likes to say that to live as the question is the antidote to everything. It's the antidote to this reality.

What would it be like to ask a question and choose to be in the question? A question empowers you to create, whereas an answer is always about how to get it right, and what you think it should look like. Coming up with the right answer eliminates the question from your reality and your life.

What if every answer or conclusion you came up with was a way of stopping you from having awareness of anything else? Like the friend that decides this guy looks right for her. Never mind that he's an alcoholic and beats her. Maybe if she can show him how much she loves him, he will change. Can you see how that could be stopping her from having the real awareness that he is choosing what he's choosing no matter how much she loves him? He may not choose to change for her or any other reason, and yet she just keeps hanging on the belief that if she just loves him enough, he will. That my friends is called unconsciousness. What if he doesn't have the capacity or desire to do so? It isn't always the case, but if she were to live as the question, she might come up with the awareness that could allow her to really choose what would be generative for her.

Living as the question looks like this in Access Consciousness®:

What is this?
What do I do with it?
Can I change it?
How do I change it?

You've heard me continuously refer to light and heavy responses to my questions. It's similar to the yes and no responses in kinesiology for those of you that know about muscle testing. It works through directly accessing the muscular feedback from your body. I teach my clients how to access a simple 'yes' or 'no' response with their bodies so they can have the conversation of what would be most generative for the body and the being in different circumstances.

In Access Consciousness®, this is referred to as light and heavy. When you ask a question, and it feels light, it's right for you. When you ask a question and it feel heavy, it's not for you. So many of these questions would elicit this response:

What is this?

Light, continue asking.

What do I do with it?

Light, continue asking.

Can I change it?

Heavy, not something you can change for this person in this 10 seconds.

How do I change it?

Heavy, point mute from the question above, but note, still heavy.

Then there are other questions you can live from, like these:

What is really possible here?

Light, something else is possible, so continue asking.

What question do I have here?

Light. There is something else I can ask.

What choices do I have here?

Light.

Do I choose for him, her, me? Which is light? Which is heavy?

What contribution can I be and receive here? Would staying be a contribution?
Heavy.
Would leaving?
Light.
What else is possible now?
Light.
Is it a contribution to leave now?
Light.

My best scenario for living as the question, again comes from my broken marriage. What a gift that I could easily walk away. Or in my case roll away as I still wasn't fully ambulatory when he left. How did that show up for me? It was literally moments after being settled back home from having my knee scoped on my shattered leg. I had to wait months until the multiple fractures healed before this last surgery. I had an ice pack secured around my right knee and my husband was in the kitchen banging pots and pans.

Moments later, he came around the corner with a very puzzled look on his face, and then like vomit, it came out. "I'm moving out. I need some space."

"OK." I responded still buzzed from the anesthesia, not sure where this was going.

"I can't keep taking care of you like this. I think if I move out, I'll get clearer about what I want. Not this."

56

CHOOSING HAPPINESS

Not really knowing how to respond, I could see he had already come to a conclusion about what he needed to do, but in my head I was living as the question.

What is this?
Heavy.
What do I do with it?
Heavy.
Can I change it?
Ping-ponging from light to heavy, etc.
How do I change it?
Heavy.

Although my body was uncertain as to whether I could change things in those 10 seconds, I found myself saying, "Do you want to do the work? Therapy?"

I didn't really want therapy. I knew he didn't either. But, it did elicit a response.

He yelled, "I'm tired of doing the work!" I surmised, he was referring to all the things I couldn't do from a wheelchair.

Had he heard me say the word therapy? It felt light when I asked in my head. Ok, so we both don't want therapy. Cool. Just let him vent, which he did for several moments and then he told me he had already found a place to rent. I didn't have to say or do anything else.

There was nothing I could do to change this, and so it played out.

How did I get what I wanted here without even knowing I wanted it? When I started to live as the question, things started to show up in magical ways. The more I asked, the more aware I became that there were other possibilities there I could create.

What if it was as simple as, how do you get what you want out of life? You ask questions. How do you make friends? You ask questions? How do you get laid? You ask questions. I didn't have to know anything here to create what I wanted. All I had to do is ask questions. I didn't even have to ask them out loud. How does it get any better? How easy is that?

So, how does it get any better? And now, let me share another Access Consciousness® tool that I have already mentioned several times within these pages, and will continue to do so.

HOW DOES IT GET ANY BETTER THAN THAT?

In my interesting point of view, "how does it get any better?" is a prayer and request to the Universe to show me "how," instead of me telling the Universe "how". It's the same as telling God how to do his job. "God! If you could only make me rich, then I could do so much good in the world. So, these are the ways you should go about that." And you run off your list to God. Does that sound preposterous to anyone one else?

When I live in the question of "How does it get any better than that?" the infinite, all knowing Universe begins to show me all the infinite possibilities. I can use the example of choosing to become a certified facilitator. Sometime "How does it get any better?" is a great follow-up question to "What else is possible?" As it turned out, the better option in that case was the no-interest PayPal loan. But the question didn't end there, I could have said, "Well it can't possibility get any better than that!" And then my world would have abruptly stopped. I would have created a finite, "This is the best it'll get," reality and made future possibilities impossible. Instead, other things shifted in my world and I was able to pay for the class with ease! How does it get any better than that?

So, with my ex-husband's declaration of how things weren't working for him, he was gone within a week and I could literally feel my life force coming back into my body. At first I thought I had this strange sense of fear, but I realized quickly that it was actually excitement that I was choosing to have my life back. No more cutting off my arms and legs to fit into his reality. I was choosing for me and that made me excitedly happy. A long journey was ahead of me, but I had the tools and I was well on my way.

It's all just a choice, my beautiful friends, and living as the question is the antidote to everything in this reality. Be in the question and you become the antidote and the immunization to this reality. Yes, indeed!

CHAPTER EIGHT:

NO FORM, NO STRUCTURE, NO SIGNIFICANCE

Everything you create has a life force of its own. This can be a song, a book, a recipe or a person. When I wrote my first two memoirs and put them out in the world, I noticed that they immediately began having a life of their own. As I moved on, they continued to live out in the world finding those that could appreciate what they had to say. I didn't expect my first book to be a contribution beyond being my story. Surprisingly, I got a lot of feedback from women from all walks of life that could relate to the domestic abuse aspects of my journey. My point of view when writing the book was so different. I even joke about it now saying, "If you want to learn who I am not, read this book." It's almost like my points of view didn't match my book's points of view anymore, so they had to journey on their with their own life force. The stories within had no real significance to me anymore, whereas when I wrote them, every word was significant.

Gary teases that it's like having a child. You suddenly realize your points of view no longer matter to them. They will only do what they want to do when they want to do it. And my take on that is, why place any significance on the fact that you don't share the same points of view anymore? What if the only reason your child had the points of view that matched yours is because they thought they had to, until they didn't?

When I began to realize that nothing had any real form, structure or significance, then everything suddenly became changeable in my life. I could create something different and it was easier than I thought. Suddenly, being in allowance could be a real thing. It's an altogether different thing from acceptance or tolerance. Feel how heavy those last two are in comparison?

Allowance is the space of not needing to align and agree or resist and react if someone has a different point of view. No right, no wrong, no good, no bad, no form, no structure and no significance. All I have to do is ask if it is light or heavy for me and move on. And so I share with you the next happiness tool towards freedom:

NO FORM, NO STRUCTURE, NO SIGNIFICANCE

Have you noticed how much significance we place on making something historical? Then we are never allowed, on some level, to change it. It's like making a mission statement. This is our company's mission statement that we live by, and therefore, everything we do, supports that. It cannot and will not be changed. Whew! Can you perceive just how heavy that is? Almost stoic in nature, it doesn't leave any room to create something new. What if instead we asked the question, "How long will this work for our company? Is it still relevant today?"

I first came to Nashville in 1984 to sing on a friend's album, and I never left. He moved on and I struggled with three jobs to support my music habit. I did get hired for a few commercials and became the local Gatti's Pizza girl, but nothing was supporting my bills enough to stop my other part time jobs. I eventually auditioned and landed the lead singer position for an all-girl rock band called The Paper Dolls. No one was listening to the GoGo's anymore and we were determined to surpass The Bangles in popularity. Although we had local success, I found myself, more often than not, sleeping on well-meaning strangers' couches and singing for my supper. Although we had some notable, local success, I was barely making ends meet and knew something had to change.

I took a lackey position in 1988 at a television production company that was producing solely for Entertainment Tonight. My college communications background got me the job, although it didn't mean much. I had taken too much time off between college and my dreams of being an artist to be current with film production as it was changing fast. So, I was the girl who brought my boss cigarettes, coffee and Twinkies every morning. I answered the phones and coordinated his crews on various shoots. At night, I was waiting tables at a dive bar. Time went on, and eventually I was able to quit my evening gig and work at the production company full time. I didn't realize I was getting very generative, on-the-job training simply by being there. Before I knew it, I was the main production assistant. From there, I became a director's rep, and was writing music video treatments for all the major Nashville labels. Then I naturally stepped into an executive producer position, splitting my time mainly between Nashville and Los Angeles. By 2001, the third production company I had worked for had to file for bankruptcy, and I found myself on food stamps, struggling again to make ends meet.

Talk about living in 10-second increments and following the energy, and all before real Internet. Friends loaned me money to pay my bills as I struggled to get on my feet again. My mother gave me $100 to create a business bank account and to start my own production company and I got my first break when a now long-time friend awarded me a Mindy McCready video. Capitol Records paid upfront for the video, which was unheard of, and I was able to pay off all my new office equipment and pay back my friends for helping me out.

Within my first year, I made six figures and was one of the two female executive producers of music videos and short films. How did I get so lucky? I look back at the last few paragraphs and wonder whose life I'm talking about, and all this before I was married in 2003.

I bet you are beginning to wonder where is the example of no form, no structure, no significance? Does any of my story have any form, structure or significance? I suppose I could have dug my heels in and declared that I was an artist and shouldn't be schlepping coffee and working overtime hours putting together production crews for other artists. I suppose I could have had an interesting point of view being a college educated girl, waiting tables, but I didn't place any significance on what my life was supposed to look like. I just knew that through it all, I was a happy camper. My life wasn't boring and I managed to create and recreate myself over and over without a roadmap as to what it was supposed to look like. Funny, I see myself as a structured individual when it comes to keeping my world in order. But with all of this, there was chaos and that was the creative aspect that got me past what others might have thought was crazy. No, I didn't have a plan. I just followed the energy.

I found myself in the space of continually asking, "Who or what can I contribute to today? Where should I put my attention now? What's contributing the most to me?"

At the top of my game, the bottom fell out again. Record labels were failing or consolidating. A new brand of directors became the first entrepreneurs of music videos that were creating masterpieces on high 8 instead of film, and for a lot less. As you know, now anyone can make a quality video on their iPhone. But, I digress for one moment. The example is clear. The film industry had to change with the changing technology. They couldn't stay within the same perimeters any longer and thrive. I saw many film production companies either greatly down-size or go belly up.

Me? I had a great run. I went from a beat-up Nissan to a Porsche convertible in the course of my film production career.

What if everything that worked for you before, stopped working for you? Things change with jobs, relationships, bodies; it's ongoing. Sticking with something because you always have limits you.

No form, no structure, and no significance means you cannot be confined by anything. Significance becomes limitation. It's just a point of view, which means you can change it.

CHAPTER NINE:

NO JUDGEMENT, NO DISCRIMINATION, NO DISCERNMENT

Have you noticed how much judgement is going on in our world right now? Just turn on the TV and everyone seems to be pointing the finger at someone else. The no-tolerance level appears to be at an all-time high. Notice the heaviness of the word, tolerance; and yet as heavy as that word is, put 'no' in front of it and the people spin out. What if instead, we could choose to be in allowance. Which if you'll recall, is more about not being hooked by others choices, opinions and judgements. Remember, it doesn't mean you have to align and agree or even choose those points of view.

It's as if the world is operating on the premise that we can't live this life without judgements. No wonder nobody appears to be happy. How could they be?

Gary explains it this way: Doing judgement is like convicting yourself of a life sentence and the effects of that judgement for the eternity of your life and others you may interact with as well. It's like a bad infection. In other words, if you worry about how people judge you, or you decide you don't like to be judged, you will be stuck in a life sentence of the effects. Look at our current leaders in the White House. Our president is the king of judgement and, yet, won't tolerate being judged.

Every judgement eliminates the capacity and awareness to perceive anything that does not match it. As soon as you buy a judgement as real, you come to a conclusion about it. In that space, how could one possibly see that there really could be another choice available?

And here's the next tool to happiness I'd like to share to free you up from your no-choice reality:

NO JUDGEMENT, NO DISCRIMINATION, NO DISCERMENT

If you have no judgement, no discrimination and no discernment, you give yourself the space to choose something different.

Let's try a little experiment. Feel the energy of judgment. What do you perceive? Heavy? Light? Indifferent? Now, tap into the energy of pure awareness. Expand out and include everything. What do you perceive now? Heavy? Light? Indifferent?

Now consider that not everything that is negative is a judgement and not everything that's positive is not, not a judgment. How's that possible? Even a compliment

CHOOSING HAPPINESS

can be considered a judgement, but what if the judgement was along the lines of, "That sweater really looks good on you. It hides your double chin." Now, is that compliment light, or did it become heavy? Now, if you can perceive it as just an interesting point of view that you don't have to align and agree with, or resist and react to, does the energy of it yet change again? Go back to feeling the energy of judgement without the point of view that it's negative or positive. Just perceive the energy of judgement and notice what you sense. For me, judgement always had a density to it until I took away the need for the judgement to be positive or negative and simply received it as an interesting point of view. Then it became neutral without heaviness or lightness. Now, perceive the energy of pure awareness. My experience of awareness is that it always has a lightness to it.

Dr. Dain Heer says something I like quite a lot. "Awareness includes everything and excludes nothing, without judgements, including judgements." Maybe you find that there are certain things you simply would not choose for your life. That's fine. But what if you could simply see it for what it is, then perhaps you could begin to perceive it as not necessarily a judgement. Notice the energy of it. If someone is mean to you, then from this space you can now perceive that they are just a mean person. It's just their personality and it has nothing to do with you. That's what awareness is. It's a place where you recognize that a person is mean without a judgment about it. That's just who they are.

Perhaps it's time I share another useful tool called expanding out. What is expanding out? It's a process I teach when I facilitate meditation classes, although it is something you can achieve without a formal sitting practice. Over the years I have facilitated for hundreds of never before meditators to get to a place beyond what they ever imagined, with ease. I'll give you an idea of what that looks like now, and you can even participate with your eyes open while reading the words. How does it get any better?

Take a couple of deep breaths, breathing in for the count of four and out for the count of eight. Sitting comfortably, imagine that there is a string attached to the top of your head, and your body is simply dangling underneath. Allow your body to go soft and your shoulders to melt away from your ears. Let go! Let go even more! Now imagine that with your next in-breath you are breathing in awareness, however that shows ups for you. It may be a sensation, a warming feeling, a sound, a taste or maybe a color that permeates your body. Have no judgement of how it shows up for you and simply be a witness to it. Continue to breath-in this awareness and allow it to begin filling all the cells of your body. Continue this way, breathing in more and more awareness until your body is full of this delicious, vibrating awareness. And finally, when you feel as though you are completely full, allow this awarenesses to seep through the pores of your body and fill the room you are in. So now you are no longer just inside your body, your body is inside of you. Can you perceive how aware you are now? Can you sense how expanded you've become?

In the classes I facilitate, I take the student all the way to the ethers which in my world I call infinite being land. And from this energy, space and consciousness, my entire world is inside of me. I am no longer in a reality that is seemingly dense and heavy, but rather I am including everything in my expanded state and all problems disappear. This is what it is to be a walking and talking meditation my friends. Although this is a juicy exercise in a sitting practice with eyes closed, what is so amazing is that you can live in this state, functioning in this reality and from here you can easily perceive that which is heavy or light for you. Imagine all the infinite possibilities you could create and generate from that space.

As my little gift to you, I've included a link to a short recording of the expanding out meditation. Should you want the full-length, deliciously milked version, you could host me for a class. What else is possible now?

So, let's get back to "No judgement, no discrimination and no discernment." Right as I got to this particular chapter in the book, I got an email from one of my clients who criticized the way I conducted myself while teaching one of my classes. She implied I was very unprofessional and hurtful in my delivery and her intention was to not judge but to share her thoughts. The entire 200-word essay was a criticism of how I did things and criticism is just another form of judgement. Most people see their judgements as just their points of view.

The reality of it for me is, a point of view is just a point of view. In most cases, I perceive people using their points of view as a way of controlling others. Impelling your point of view is still judgement, but if I can see it as an interesting point of view, that's all it is for me. It doesn't stick me. My awareness was that she had very interesting points of view about the way I teach. My point of view is that I'm not going to sugar-coat and go down the rabbit hole with my clients. Not on my watch. I make that clear with my clients in the beginning. That said, I'm not for everyone. Does it stick me? No. It doesn't matter how much someone might try to impel me with their interesting point of views and the rightness of them, especially when it's directed at me. How freeing. Judge me all you want. I am aware that it's simply your point of view. Not right, not wrong, not good and not bad.

When you're in the space of defending your points of view, which are really just your judgements, it's a vicious life sentence that creates nothing generative, different or new in your life. When you discriminate and discern which judgements are right or wrong, or good or bad, which ones you can receive and which ones you cannot, you lock yourself out of any joy you could be choosing. Would you rather be stuck in the right-ness of your point of view or would you rather have the lightness of pure awareness that includes everything and excludes nothing, including judgement? It's just a choice, my beautiful friends. Will you choose it?

CHAPTER TEN:

NO DRUGS

Is your head spinning yet? Still with me? Good! Take a deep breath. If you've come this far with me, then perhaps some of this is making sense. There are so many other things that could distract you from this book, so please acknowledge that you've come this far. Thank you.

I met my college boyfriend when he was tripping on acid. That would be my first encounter with the severe effects drugs could have on someone. In my experience, I had never been that close to an addict. Maybe my happy-go-lucky self was more than a little naive. After missing my first class in college, I was very aware of all the college campus alcohol abuse, and would always smell pot at concerts, but when I noticed these cartoons on paper being passed around and people putting them in their mouths, naive or not, I didn't go there. Don't get me wrong. I had my share of experimenting and nothing stuck. I especially hated marijuana and still do. Why would I want to take anything that took me completely out of my awareness? The rare times I allowed my boyfriend to talk me into smoking pot, I just got paranoid and disoriented, then usually over ate and over slept. Maybe I was lucky that I wasn't into it. He was not so lucky and suffered with drug addiction his entire life. His sister recently reached out to me on Facebook to let me know he had passed away in his early fifties from a heart attack.

I hope you can perceive the choice here over the point of view in my next tool I would like to share. Drugs just don't work for me. It's not that I have an opinion about what others choose here. It just doesn't work for me. That said, it also doesn't work for me in a relationship. So my next tool to being joyful is:

NO DRUGS OF ANY KIND

What are drugs? Well, that's a wide net. It not only includes the now legalized recreational drugs I'm not personally fond of, but it also includes non-legal street drugs, legal prescription drugs, alcohol (some would argue) anything addictive. For me, anything that pulls me out of my awareness does not work for me. Does that mean I won't have a martini or two on occasion? No. But, would it work for me to drink like my boyfriend in college did, throwing up and not remembering anything we did the night before? No. That was pure unconsciousness. I'm sure there are a lot of people who are happy when they are doing anything that could be mind-altering. It's when you do drugs to get happy that it can be tricky. I'm sure Ed never thought the drugs would eventually kill him. I'm sure Michael Jackson and Prince thought the same thing. Fortunately, there are different protocols in place for those that wish to choose something different like Alcoholics Anonymous and Narcotics Anonymous, plus all the other groups in place for families to cope and eventually thrive. But there is a lot more at stake here.

Drugs create a bio-chemical personality, so when someone chooses drugs they are choosing to become a certain type of personality. It is my interesting point of view that a lot of people choose drugs to drown out their awareness; after all, would an infinite being choose to get high? No. They would choose awareness. I get it. Sometimes all this awareness can make your butt itch. But, if you can live in awareness as an interesting point of view, you don't have the point of view that you need to drown anything out. I have some clients that feel that all this so-called awareness is just too darn intense for them. Many of those clients are on depression medications. The caveat is that when you do drugs to tone down your awareness, it actually exponentializes awareness, like acid does. It puts everything into the sensory cortex of the brain, and the cruel joke is, now you find yourself being reactive in areas of your life where you normally wouldn't be. It's like sensory over-load that can't be controlled. So the thing you were try-ing to control becomes uncontrollable and takes more to gain control over, and the cycle continues. Have you seen drug users that are addicted, but say they are not? They say they can function, although it's like they are on automatic pilot, going unconscious more and more until the light just goes out.

If you are doing drugs of any kind, you cannot choose consciousness. Instead you are choosing, what Gary and Dr. Dain call, anti-consciousness. It is not that drugs are wrong, The problem with most drugs is they open the door to entities or demons coming into your body. I have had clients that couldn't remember any-thing after they had their first drink and even won-dered how they got home, waking up just fine the next day, but with no memory. In these cases, it's been my experience that they have been taking drug and alcohol entities into their bodies and allowing themselves to go on auto-pilot, checking out completely until it's last call for alcohol. Somehow they get home, seemingly unscathed, and the entities or demons move on. That's what I call an "open door policy." These clients even claim that something is telling them to have a drink, or two or more, until they can't remember anymore. When they appear to still be in the body, it becomes ap-parent that many of these entities don't even know they are dead and they are just searching out the vibration they knew when they had a body. Perhaps they died of a drug overdose or alcohol related accident.

Now, let me be clear here. My point of view is not that alcoholism is just a delivery system for drug and alcohol entities to feel like they have a body again. They can't even get in unless the host is unconscious. It's just one of the possibilities why someone might feel the uncontrollable urge to drink.

"No Drugs" does not mean that you stop taking your heart medication or insulin. I have standard prescriptions that I take for allergies. The thing is, I talk to my body and ask it daily if it would be generative to continue to take the medications. Presently it is, although I am working with a homeopath with the target of vibrationally eliminating my Tennessee allergies. The joke may be on me. You could say that I am really allergic to this reality. How do I change that? Interesting point of view my body has that point of view, and believe me, I'm using that tool as well.

I am, as are all of us, a multidimensional being with multiple energetic bodies that are not physical. Consider etheric, subtle, causal, etc. Your entire body will crave energy it requires to bypass whatever it is that is limiting it. In homeopathy, you take away whatever is creating the limitation by bringing up these blockages, and then the need for the drug or craving dissipates and disappears.

It is proven that if you take more of a drug than the body can utilize, it doesn't dissipate fully and stores it in the fat cells. This is especially true of pain medications and sleep aids. This is called a half-life. For example: The half-life of Ambien is about 2 hours. If you took a 10mg Ambien tablet at 8pm then by 10pm there would be 5mg remaining in your system and by 12pm there would be 2.5mg in your system and so on. Then it releases when you get enough of the catalyst that will release it again. That is the reason that pot and some opiates stay in the body's system for up to 14 days. Imagine daily usage of these drugs and what that would create in the body, besides unconsciousness?

When I met my ex-husband, he was a very high strung, anxiety ridden being and he relied on Ambien to help him retire at night. There were several occasions where he would take it before the news finished, and would pass out in front of the TV on the couch only to wake up with the daylight. Oddly, he took it out on me for not waking him up so he could sleep in our comfortable bed. It wasn't for the lack of me trying to shake him awake, believe me. Sometimes he would mumble at me to leave him alone or, he'd be out cold and I just couldn't budge him. The times he did make it to the bed, he would sometimes experience night-terrors. One night he was still asleep and I woke up with him kicking me. I ran out of the room and slept on the couch. The next day he didn't remember a thing and I declared that I would divorce him if he didn't get off the Ambien. He switched to taking Tylenol PM and that behavior stopped, and we stayed married for the time being. This does raise the question of if there is something like an Ambien entity that searches out that energy in a being with a body. That actually feels light.

Again, this is not about having a judgement about using drugs and alcohol. It is about having the awareness that when you choose to use drugs of any kind, you are creating unconsciousness. You are then allowing the creation of a bio-chemical personality to take over your personality, and you are also creating an invitation for others without bodies to take over and run the ship. Those are just a few of the possibilities. No judgment here. I get that this has been working just fine for a lot of people and for a very long time in our history. I am aware that some people are comfortable with choosing to use drugs specifically to go unconscious from this reality. Just know that if you are one of those people it's no longer working for, you can choose differently.

RÜDRANI DEVI

CHAPTER ELEVEN:

NO COMPETITION

Through the years, I have discovered something about me, although it only shows up at very particular times. I am very competitive with myself. Being an avid runner, in the early days I did everything to get my speed up. By my third marathon, it had gotten so significant in my mind, that I was reading every book on the subject and I decided I would run the iconic Boston Marathon. With every race, I would get closer to the qualifying finish time, finally only requiring to shave off 5 precious minutes. After nine marathons, I did run my bucket-list race, but it didn't happen the way I thought it would.

I'll begin with this thought: "Would an infinite being have something they can compete with?" Each of us is as unique as a unicorn. There is no better you, than you being you. As there is no better me than the me that I be. An infinite being would choose to do competition for what reason?

And so, my next Access Consciouness® tool to happiness I would like to share is:

NO COMPETITION

Competition is a rational thought in this reality. It's the belief that if I do this against you, and beat you at it, I am better than you. I will get more attention, more fame, more money, more love, and on and on. Does that really work? No. What if you choose an irrational point of view about competition? What would that look like? For me, it's how can I out-create myself? How can I be better today than I was yesterday, with ease, joy and glory? Or what can I do to out-create you with ease, joy and glory? And yet, could we consider that competition? After all, you'll create the way you do and I'll create the way I do.

I've had people come to me and tell me that they aren't in a place to afford my services. Easily, I could say, I'm not in a place to charge you less for my services. But instead, I ask, what would be the generative contribution here? Easy! I will refer them to someone they are in a place to financially afford. Now, in this reality, that is a totally irrational point of view, simply because most people wouldn't choose it. To me it's a win-win scenario. They find a practitioner they can afford, and I leave the space open for someone who can receive my services with ease. I have also had those who come to me and tell me that if I was really "a healer" I wouldn't charge for my sessions. Interesting point of view they have that point of view. And I move on. I don't find the need to justify my position. I acknowledge and am very grateful for the work that I do. I'm in a very generative space where I don't have to worry about creating clients in my practice. In fact, most will ask me when they should come back and see me, and my answer to them is to ask your body. There is true freedom and happiness in not being needy or competitive regarding a totally booked schedule. On the rare occasion that I have an unexpected day off, I put my attention to other tasks or maybe that's a day I get to spoil myself. How can I out-spoil myself today that would make me super joyful right away?

I absolutely love Gary's point of view regarding competition. He says that each one of us is more unique than we even know. We are the Hope diamond of consciousness, but we have defined ourselves as the hopeless diamond of our personal realities. The truth is, each of us is the only one of our kind. We are all unique. We are all different. In other words, what I do is different from what anybody else can or will do. And, what you do is different from what anybody else can or will do. We have to be willing to recognize that. There is no one who can compete with you, so why are you bothering to compete? In my interesting point of view, it always works against me as I'll begin judging myself that I'm not doing enough.

When I was in film production, representing music video directors, there would be several film production companies' directors vying for the same music video. More times than not, I had two directors under my roof competing for the same project. What was always interesting is if one of my directors would be awarded the video over the other, inevitably, the one not chosen would have points of view about the other's music video treatment. Judgements? Well, not always. Sometimes it was simply an awareness of why the artist and record label went with her concept over his. Her version may have simply been a better fit in those 10 seconds. Don't get me wrong. My directors were very competitive. They wanted to be awarded the job and get more attention, more money, etc. But, each of the video directors I represented, all had very different talents and abilities that were unique to them. I was very lucky to be able to represent such talented and amazing, albeit, diverse beings, truly.

I remember Dr. Dain once asking, "Would an infinite being have someone they can compete with?" In order to create competition as a reality, you would first, out of necessity have to create yourself as a limited, finite being. Feel how solid that is? Infinite verses finite? When you're being the infinite being that you truly be, you get to choose your life. When you pretend to be a finite being, you solidify the only choice you think you have in this reality. So instead of competing, what if acknowledging the one of a kind, infinite being that you truly be and simply out-create yourself. Maybe do competition with yourself instead of others, which isn't real anyway. Then you can bloom and grow even more than you thought possible. Doesn't that feel like a joyful way to do competition if you had to do it?

I am so grateful for my ex-husband. He's created some great examples in this book for me. How does it get any better? He loved to do competition, especially with me. He worked for Country Music Television and was excellent at his job. If we were competing to create the best commercial to get viewers, I would surmise that he would have out-created me more times than not. I never had the opportunity to find this out, nor did I desire it. He, on the other hand, wanted to compete with me on every level. He was the best at mowing the lawn, making dinner, doing laundry, parking the car, and he always let me know it. Was any of that really true in my reality? No. My awareness was simply that he mowed the grass differently than I did, made dinner differently than I did, and had a different point of view about doing the laundry or parking the car. The one that made his butt itch was when he decided he was going to be a runner.

We went to all the elite running stores and bought him all the fancy gear 'real runners' would use. I noticed that he bogarted my heart monitor, insisting that he needed it more than I did. Well, that awareness was actually spot on. He would use my head bands and eventually the cumbersome mile tracker that he had purchased as a Christmas present for me. He wanted so much to be better at everything than me that he even had to be a better looking runner. He read my books and looked online for tips. Did that make him a better runner? Well, he did have a lot of points of view about how we should train. Because I had been doing kinesiology for several years already, I would ask my body what worked for it. That went from what would be the most generative running gear, what to eat, to length of runs and how fast we should pace ourselves. Gary says, sometimes ya just gotta do what's easier even if you don't agree with it. And for me, the easier thing was letting him train us for the Nashville Country Music 1/2 Marathon. Granted, I had already run it three times as marathon training runs, and crashed it when I needed an even longer training run than 13.1 miles.

He even solicited other CMT employees to run it with us. T-shirts were made and money was raised. It became an event within the event. And then the day came for the race. He had never trained over 7 miles because the running book he chose to base our training on didn't suggest it, whereas I was running 12 miles every Friday. I had asked my body if this book would work for us and got a 'no' so, when we didn't train together, I did my own thing.

We stayed together as far as six miles and then I noticed that he was slowing down. "Are you fatigued?" I asked.

"No, beloved. I have to pee," he answered.

"Well go ahead. I'll wait."

"No, I'll catch up with you. You keep running."

So I did. I kept pace, which was like a typical Friday run for me. When I crossed the finish line, I hung close and grabbed a banana and some water to hand him. I was a bit surprised to see a lot of our CMT group arrive before he did, as I knew we were way ahead of most of them from the start. When he eventually showed up, he was breathing hard. I told him how proud I was of him for running his first half marathon. He basked in his accomplishment and I doted on him even more with his CMT co-workers.

I gotta hand it to him, he stuck it out. And although he would mention more than once that he could have beat me if he wanted to, he did acknowledge that due to his bathroom break, I "won, fair and square," even though he could see that I sprinted away from him. I didn't realize that there would be a winner and loser running this race together. He had told me that he wanted us to spend more time together, and made the decision to do the race. My pace at the six-mile marker was certainly not a sprint, but alas, what an interesting point of view.

I got the energy of his interesting point of view that day, and it was from that point forward that I became aware of how people only accuse you of being competitive if they are being competitive. He basically accused me of what he was actually doing. It was a great awareness that continues to come in handy.

I remember smiling at this new-found awareness. I thought to myself, regardless of all the races I had run before we even met, he knew I was a more efficient and faster runner than he was. And he just indirectly told me so without even knowing it himself. Isn't awareness grand?

CHAPTER TWELVE:

DO NOT LISTEN TO, TELL, OR BUY THE STORY

Everyone loves a good story-teller, or do they? Of course there is always the guy who can hold a room captive with his outlandish or funny musings. Everyone likes that guy and if they throw a party, they make sure he's invited for added entertainment.

What about those people that when we see them coming, we want to run the other way? Think Saturday Night Live's Debbie Downer. Oh wait, she was entertaining and funny too!

I'm talking about those people who are consistently the object of everything. Some of those people are the same ones who wanted to know what I was so happy about. So, let's get into this further with this next Access Consciousness® tool:

DO NOT LISTEN TO, TELL, OR BUY THE STORY

What if stories were justifications for the interesting points of view you made about something to prove you were right? "Because this happened, I had to do this. I had no other choice." Really? Stories are justifications for the limitations people are choosing, as though they had no other choice. So, what if the story was just the story. It's not reality and it's not the truth. What if it didn't really mean anything?

What if the story is how you justify the limitations of your life and your reality? I have a close family friend that maintains her story so that she can maintain her victimhood. It allows her to justify the choices that she made, rather than acknowledge that she actually chose it to begin with. It was the holidays, and there were several friends mingling after singing carols and having holiday punch. I was within earshot of her story about how she had made less money that year than she had paid in taxes. I heard all her reasons why this happened, because of this and because of that. It was as if she didn't want to choose to live her life. She would rather choose all the reasons why she couldn't. She went from being to being, telling her story to anyone that would listen, until it was my turn.

"I heard all about it." I said after she started. "Evidently it's your new mantra."

Now why would I want to wedgie a family friend? I wasn't working and she wasn't paying me for my awareness. Maybe I thought it would be funny. It did put a funny look on her face.

"Well, it's what happened," she said justifying her point of view.

"OK, cool." And I let it lie. I didn't want to get into it as I wasn't sure she could receive it. And after all, it was just my awareness. It didn't really mean anything.

I suppose it sounded like a judgement to her as, after screwing up her face few times, she asked, "What do you mean by that?"

"Well, you know I'm joking about the mantra thing." I was back-peddling now, sussing out the energy of it to see where I could go with it or if I even should.

"It's not funny. It's what happened." She looked at me blankly. "Help me understand."

I studied her face. Was she getting ready to attempt to gaslight me? Or did I note a spark of awareness in those eyes. It felt light, so I proceeded.

"Well," I cautiously began, "Did you ever consider that sharing your private, perhaps not so pleasant, matter with everyone might be uncomfortable for them?" I paused, "And, now that they know, would it be possible that this might create more of the same reality for you? If you persist with the same story, you get them to buy your story of lack as true for you, and that's going to be their perceived continued point of view of who you are. Do you really want them to perceive you as struggling?"

She didn't say a word, but she was captivated.

"Sanskrit mantras are usually positive statements that one wishes to achieve. It's of my opinion that you probably don't want to create making less than you paid in taxes ever again, so why would you want to repeat this sad story to anyone and everyone who will listen?" Her eyes shifted a second and I could sense that she was actually contemplating that as a possibility.

"I didn't realize I was doing that."

"Well, no judgement here," I replied. "It's just my awareness. Maybe changing that for you would be to not buy your own story about it, so you could possibly create something different."

"But it's what happened."

"I get it." I answered. "But what if you could create something different next time? Not get stuck in the 'because' of your story? It's just a choice. You can choose differently next time. "

Her mouth didn't move, but her eyes were inquisitive.

"You'd be surprised how quickly the simple question of 'what else is possible here' can turn things around."

We chatted for a while longer and then the party broke up and we said our farewells. Several years later, I understand that things have indeed turned around for her with her work situation, and she even bought a second home, renting the first one out as segmented apartments. How does it get any better than that?

That was a lucky break for me in that I was able to hold the space of a conversation that could have gone south quickly. I've learned not to share my observations unless I can perceive that it really can be received. If it can't, it's not a kindness to go there.

Back in the day, I was a big justifier for sure. Namely, it was for objects or things I wanted that I would justify why I needed that object or thing and feel I had to explain why. I'm sure y'all have heard the one about champagne taste on a beer budget. Well, I like nice things, nice meals and nice vacations. Talk about justifications to allow myself to have these things in my life. Usually a trip was not just a trip. It was a trip where I had to tack on a business meeting to justify taking any time off to make my story valid. It also made me look like a good employee. Crazy point of view, but at the time, that's what I chose. What if I didn't have to make my story as true and real? What if I didn't have to have a reason why? What if I could take a vacation because I could? No right. No wrong.

I remember working as a sales rep for a fulfillment company. We sold packaging and duplication of VHS, 3/4" and BetaMax tapes. Yes, I realize how I just dated myself. I was a sales rep for the music industry, but I wanted to branch out to the gaming market.

Magically, I had an opportunity, wherein a friend was going to London for work and had a non-refundable companion ticket. We would need to stay in the same room as the hotel was booked up, but I justified that as saving money. At least, that's how I told it to my current boyfriend. Although this guy and I had dated before, I surmised that we were more mature now, and happily in other relationships. You see, there was this huge gaming company I had been romancing over the phone that would let me fly back with the master for a very large order. How could I not go? I presented this to my boss, who, although he agreed, wondered how my boyfriend would feel about it.

Let's just say, as the major justifier I was at that time, I had zero tools for this situation. I called my boyfriend, who was a road manager for a very high profile artist, so he wasn't even home. I would be leaving before they got back from that leg of the tour. I told him of my good fortune and thought, surely he would be happy and agree that this was indeed an opportunity I couldn't pass up.

"Well, you got it all figured out, don't you." He said very quietly.

"Wow!" I was so excited. "Thank you so much for understanding!"

I called my friend back and he arranged everything. You see, the name on the other ticket would need to be changed to my name. I wasn't sure how he was going to do it, but as he was a high-powered promotor for Warner Bros. Records, I assumed he could make things like that happen. Again, the magic was aligning for me.

Now, I'm sure this is sounding like a much lighter story than my family friend's, but is it really? I could pretend all I wanted that my boyfriend was going to be OK with this trip, but that was me choosing to not choose awareness, and I sank deeper into all the reasons why I just had to go.

It wasn't until I was on the plane that I got the rest of Bill's story. He was going to take his girlfriend on this business trip, but she wanted to take a break and he had this non-refundable ticket. When he told her who he was taking instead, she knew we had been intimate before and that didn't go very well. As for the rest of my story, after I got home my boyfriend broke up with me.

Although, nothing rekindled on that trip between my friend and me, looking back on it now, what we did was not a kindness to either one of our partners. He and I knew nothing was going to happen between us. We split amicably knowing we were better as friends than lovers. Did our partners know that? Well, I'm sure that even with us telling them that, they wouldn't be able to receive it.

What if instead I had said something along the lines of, "Honey, I have this business opportunity to go to London to meet up with my first potential gaming client. It's all paid for and I'll only be gone a week. How fabulous is that?" It would have been accurate without all the justifications for why he should buy my story as my only choice. Or better yet, "Honey, I'm going to London for business and because I can, I'm extending my trip. I'll be back in a week."

Instead, giving him something he could not receive, I inadvertently rubbed in his face that my ex-boyfriend had this extra ticket that was going to go to waste, so I should take advantage of that and pursue this client. Sure, he would be able to receive that. Not at all. And that, my friends, was not a kindness. And it certainly was not honoring of our relationship. Hind-sight, folks.

I imagine some of you might have the point of view that not telling him the entire story would not be a kindness either. But it didn't actually happen like that anyway. The point is, there were other kinder choices I could have made if I wasn't so invested in repeating my story for validity, telling my story to anyone who would listen, and then wanting everyone to buy the story so I wouldn't have to feel bad about taking a vacation.

I only got one of those days as a work day. I used the rest of the week days as vacation days. I did get the client and several really big commission orders, although I'm certain an infinite being would have done things differently. At that time, I just wasn't that into awareness. I was more into competition and what was in it for me. Today things are very different. I may have been wired for joy back then, but the difference between my happiness now and then is that today, it's authentic happiness.

Have you ever noticed that people who are really into the story are usually not really into awareness? Interesting point of view they have that point of view. Been there. Done that. No judgement. It's just a choice.

CHAPTER THIRTEEN:

NO EXCLUSION

Could an infinite being exclude anyone or anything from their life? Awareness includes everything and excludes nothing, warts and all and without judgement. You can't do awareness and exclusion at the same time. It's impossible. So, in order to be aware, you have to do inclusion.

And the last tool I'm going to share with you on your journey to authentic happiness, is this one:

NO EXCLUSION

Exclusion is a way to shut others out completely. An infinite being would choose to exclude others for what reason? What if exclusion was actually excluding the person from coming into your life and being totally present with you? It doesn't mean that you have to give them anything. It's about being able to receive them as they are whether you align and agree or resist and react to them. Doing this does not mean that they will come into your life. This might not be something they have the capacity to choose. An infinite being holds the space for that with no judgement. Even if people shut you out of their reality or their life, it doesn't mean you don't allow them to be included in yours.

It's odd that on a few occasions, I have been asked if I would ever facilitate for a terrorist. Interesting question. I've also got the usual suspects of "would you facilitate for a child molester or a rapist?" The short answer is yes. Aside from an infinite being including everyone and excluding no one, what if I'm the only shot for this person to become aware of their actions and perhaps wish to choose something different? Why wouldn't I want to help create that in their world? Wouldn't this small act of kindness make this world a lighter place for all of us? Dare I say, what would Jesus do?

Now, I'm not going to give up my awareness in all of this. If there is a sense of clear and present danger, then my choices of how I facilitate, if at all, could be different. How many therapists facilitate prisoners in a safe environment? Gary says, you cannot honestly facilitate anyone if you have a point of view about them, because your point of view will stick you. If you find you have a point of view, the kindest thing you could do is give them to another therapist.

Again, if I had the awareness that this person wasn't being truthful, or could hurt someone very badly if they were granted parole, then as an infinite being, that would be the awareness I would put in my report. Knowing that, would an infinite being say, "I just can't facilitate this person because they are bad?" I'll let you answer this time. If I were to dismiss this being as someone I shouldn't waste my time on, I would be cutting off my awareness. Instead, if I were to include them in my world, I would also have the awareness of what the most generative action would be, even if it's death. An infinite being doesn't have a point of view either way. An infinite being simply chooses based on what her choices could create. It's that simple.

I recently got a call from a reflexology client of mine that I hadn't seen since I had facilitated for her husband with Parkinson's. Years had gone by and now she wanted me to facilitate for her middle-aged son. He had been a prominent chiropractor in Nashville years before with a reputable practice and was well revered by the holistic community. By demand, he had moved his practice to LA and that's when, according to her, he spun out of control.

He had decided that he wanted to specialize in addiction, but wanted a clearer understanding of what that was. So over the course of several weeks, he experimented with different psychedelics eventually adding heroine to his experience. Unmonitored, things did not go as he had hoped and his practice exploded. He began taking addicts into his parents' LA home. Still in Nashville, they were unaware of all of this until they walked into their trashed residence, face to face with their son's drug-addicted girlfriend. There's a lot more to this story, although this is enough for you to get the energy of it.

By the time she called me, he had a near-death episode after a yelling match with his girlfriend. They were on the top level of a parking garage. She left him standing in the garage, tripping. After more screaming, he ran right off the top of the parking garage. When the ambulance came, he wasn't dead, but they didn't expect him to live. As his injuries were life threatening, instead of a psych ward, he went into intensive care.

Due to the nature of his care, he got clean but was never the same. At the time, I was getting my home remodeled, so I was living in an apartment close by. His mother told me that he said he had demons and wanted them exorcised, something I have a talent and ability to clear. After a very brief chat, he was on his way to me. I cracked the sliding glass door just in case he started screaming and left the apartment door unlocked as well. I had the panic alarm key fob in my office in case I had to use it, and then there was my mobile phone nearby as well. The minute he walked in, I could sense that he wasn't alone. There wasn't any record of him hurting anyone but himself, so far. I was going to be sure I wasn't the first.

I expanded out into infinite being land so that I could be acutely aware and ready for anything. He quickly announced that he was God and that he could easily erase my feeble mind so that I could be happy in this world that had gone into the shitter.

"That's what I get for giving these people free will!" he barked.

"Thank you for the offer," I said, acknowledging him, "but I'm good with my feeble mind at the moment. Please have a seat and tell me why you're here."

Thus, began a tirade of screaming that turned into tears and then suddenly like a child, he became docile. I followed along as each entity revealed itself to me and expanded out more to include them all. It was a lot and, in hindsight, I would have probably referred his mother to Dr. Dain and Gary. As it was, it wasn't until the hour-long conversation I had with his mother after the session, that I did so.

I managed to get him on my table a few times. Each time I would touch him to release these demons, he would jump off screaming that I was hurting him. One time he said I set him on fire. I did manage to remove three entities during our session, but there was a lot more going on and he wasn't ready to have them all evacuate. They gave him a false sense of power that was very significant to him. Once I discovered the portal, I was stuck. Unless he wanted to close it, there was no way it was going to happen. At least I wasn't aware of a way to make that happen.

I talked the child down into whispers and then announced that I was very sorry that I couldn't help him more. His demeanor changed, and his eyes glazed over as he looked right through me. Then he announced matter-of-factly, "That's OK kid. You tried." He patted me on the head. "I'll send you the bill."

And like that, he was gone. I called his mother to give her a heads-up and we made arrangements to talk later.

Two hours had gone by, and yet barely anything had shifted in his world. The little bit that I could facilitate came from a place of total inclusion, and I imagine that, in some small way, this was the first time he felt he had been heard in a long time.

Was he crazy out of his mind? Yes. That's my awareness. Did he really want change? My awareness said no. Did I have a point of view about it? No. Did I feel like a failure? No.

This experience was such a gift to me. It showed me that I could hold the space from a no judgment place even if it hadn't proven to be a success in his reality. In mine, it was. I don't know if I could have held the space even two years before. I found myself to be strangely at peace with the outcome.

If I had excluded him, unable to receive him, I wouldn't have had the awareness to hold the space for him. Awareness includes everything and excludes nothing. Now I knew what that really was. Do I still struggle with this tool? Well, the short answer is, when it comes to family, yes. It has become apparent that even though I do deeply honor my family and am grateful for the way they show up, it is sometimes difficult for me to include them in my world. In the past I found myself doing "interesting point of view" a lot. Today it happens very infrequently. My family is a very generative trigger to keep me in my awareness. It's something I deeply desire to create in my life so that I can truly be in a space of no judgement. Mostly so I can be in no judgement of myself. What else is possible now?

I am improving though. Christmas of 2017 was the best yet. I had this terrible sinus thing going on and even had canceled performing in back-to-back shows shortly before. One thing I haven't mentioned thus far is that I am a singer and performer and play electric violin and some percussion for a few local Nashville-based bands. After fully healing my body from the terrorist attacks, I decided to out-create myself by doing whatever created joy for me no matter what. Singing is definitely one of the most joyous things I do and was the main reason I first came to Nashville, lovingly coined as Music City. And I am immensely grateful that there are those that support my love of performing by attending our shows, but I digress.

Now back to Christmas of 2017. My older sister was getting married, and I couldn't wait to take photos and make her and her betrothed a Shutterfly Book, one of my addictions. Everything felt light for the first time in years.

Was I just choosing it?

CHAPTER FOURTEEN:

ARE YOU READY TO CHOOSE?

What if you didn't live in this reality? What if this reality lived in you?

Dr. Dain posed this curious questions during an "Ask" tele-call, which was followed up with a "Receive" tele-call. Even though it's right there in the Bible, most of us don't think about asking for what we want, and then when it does show up, are we really willing to receive it?

Those two tele-calls changed my perception of how I lived in this world. What if everything I was taught in this reality wasn't really true for me?

In that moment, I acknowledged just how much I had managed to create and generate in my life, that in this reality, hadn't really made sense that I could. I had reinvented myself so many times without even realizing it.

Just going with the flow, following the energy of whatever was light in every 10 seconds, and in most cases, not having a point of view about it. I had been ridiculed for being happy-go-lucky. And I had been asked more times than I could count, "What drugs are you on?" when I was caught smiling for apparently no reason. Was it possible that, more times than not, I simply wasn't allowing this reality to get me down? I wasn't shutting the world out at all. I just wasn't buying the story for me. Was this what it was to live in the world, but not of it?

I reconsidered everything. It wasn't that I had been wondering aimlessly through my life. I wasn't just a lucky person. I actually created my life in a reality that is seemingly impossible to navigate, supposedly. So, how had I managed? Even before Access Consciousness® and these tools I have been joyfully sharing with you, I had been defying the odds. Did I innately know something about thriving even when things in most people's worlds would have been considered gloom and doom?

And then it came to me. The truth was that I didn't receive other people's points of view as true for me. My father would tell me I was stupid and I found myself doing whatever I could to prove that I wasn't. But tell me, beautiful beings, would a stupid person have achieved as much as I had, or had as many adventures? Evidently,

I never really bought that story. And so of course I appeared naive, laughing at the state the world was in or whatever. This reality is truly funny to me. I find it interesting that people choose what they choose in their lives, and yes, that makes me laugh. They could choose differently if they wanted to. Maybe they don't know that or maybe they are comfortable in their choices, even when they appear to be unhappy with their lot in life. I'm in allowance of their choices even if they wouldn't work for me. It doesn't make them right or wrong. It's just a choice. And, it doesn't make me innocent or naive at all to be in the space of "interesting choice." It's called awareness. Instead of seeing the effects of our world as right or wrong, I have this awareness that this is what our world is choosing. Interesting choice, granted, but that is how situations are created. We choose. Do we always choose consciously? No, mostly not, in my awareness.

So getting back to this happiness piece. What if you could just choose it? What if it was as easy as saying, "I'll have that!" A friend recently asked me what I wanted for my birthday, and my answer was, to be even more joyful than I already am! Tag line? And jewelry is nice, too! Hey, I am a girl y'all. But, all kidding aside, YES, I CHOOSE HAPPINESS. It beats the alternative. And it is my wish for all of you reading this book that you will consider the same. It's just a choice. The only question remaining is, *will you choose it*?

RÜDRANI DEVI

ABOUT THE AUTHOR:

Rüdrani Devi is an authentic Shaman, descending from generations of gifted women within her family lineage. Considered a medical intuitive in the healing community, she studied and became a certified vibrational healer through the National Institute of Health in Boulder Colorado in 2004.

Presently, Devi conducts remote and in-person energy sessions from her practice in Nashville, TN. She is also available for speaking engagements and book signings, and offers classes in vibrational healing techniques wherever invited.

RÜDRANI DEVI

MORE ABOUT ACCESS CONSCIOUSNESS

What is Access Consciousness?

Access Consciousness® classes provide verbal processing and simple tools for change that allow as much or as little change as you are willing to choose! What if you didn't require someone else to give you an answer... just some questions that could allow you to know what you know? Would that create greater possibilities for your life?

What are The Bars®?

The first class in Access is The Bars®. Did you know there are 32 points on your head which, when gently touched, effortlessly and easily release anything that doesn't allow you to receive? These points contain all the thoughts, ideas, beliefs, emotions, and considerations that you have stored in any lifetime. This is an opportunity for you to let go of everything!

How much of your life do you spend doing rather than receiving? What if you could receive more, decrease the mind chatter and experience what it is like to be a walking, talking meditation? Receiving or learning the BARS will allow this and SO much more to show up for you! If you are truly ready for something new, this is a GREAT place to start. NO PRE-REQUISITES! How does it get any better than that?

What is the Foundation® Class?

THE FOUNDATION CLASS® is designed to empower you to change anything and everything you'd like to change in your life. You will be given a whole toolbox of tools that will allow you to break apart the foundation of limitation that we so often function from and build a new foundation, one of limitless possibility, so that you can begin to create the life you truly desire.

What do you desire? What would you like to be different? Would you like more joy? More fun? More ease? Would you like to wake up in the morning with a sense of gratitude... happy to be on the planet?

Whatever it is for you, it IS possible. Thousands of people around the world have created the life they desire by using the simple and pragmatic tools of Access Consciousness® that you will be introduced to in the Foundation class.

You will receive tools you'll use for the rest of your life. With these tools, you'll be able to have greater clarity and pragmatic new approaches to deal with limitations in relationships, money, body, sex and communication. You'll easily understand the sources of much of the miscommunication in your life, undo it and learn methods that may work MUCH better! Get FREE forever of that "money mind of chatter" in your head that goes non-stop, drives you crazy and accomplishes nothing. Learn at least two additional hands-on healing methods you can use with any prior training to heal yourself and others.

https://www.accessconsciousness.com/

SHORT DOCUMENTARY ABOUT ACCESS BARS:
https://www.youtube.com/watch?v=CB3DPofWex8&feature=share

Even more about ACCESS BARS:
https://energypsychologyjournal.org/abstracts/abstracts-volume-9-number-2-november-2017/effects-access-bars-anxiety-depression-pilot-study/

https://www.youtube.com/watch?v=5UjO-LC-RHs&feature=share

https://www.youtube.com/watch?v=p2axqedXMnw

Meaning of THE CLEARING STATEMENT:
This is an excerpt from the book, "A World of Choice. A World of Freedom" by Gary M. Douglass delineating the meaning of the Access Consciousness Clearing Statement®:

You are the only one who can unlock the points of view that have you trapped. What I am offering here is a tool you can use to change the energy of the points of view that have you locked into unchanging situations.

Throughout this book ("A World of Choice. A World of Freedom"), I ask a lot of questions, and some of those questions might twist your head around a little bit. That's my intention. The questions I ask are designed to get your mind out of the picture so you can get to the energy of a situation.

Once the question has twisted your head around and brought up the energy of a situation, I ask if you are willing to destroy and uncreate that energy__becuase stuck energy is the source of barriers and limitations. Destroying and uncreating that energy will open the door to new possibilities for you.

This is your opportunity to say, "Yes, I'm willing to let go of whatever is holding that limitation in place."

That will be followed by some weird-speak we call the clearing statement:

Right and Wrong, Good and Bad, POD and POC, All 9, Shorts, Boys and Beyonds®

With the clearing statement, we're going back to the energy of the limitations and barriers that have been created. We're looking at the energies that keep us from moving forward and expanding into all of the spaces that we would like to go, The clearing statement addresses the energies that are creating the limitations and contraction in our life.

The more you run the clearing statement, the deeper it goes and the more layers and levels it can unlock for you. If a lot of energy comes up for you in response to a question, you may wish to repeat the process numerous times until the subject being addressed is no longer an issue for you.

You don't have to understand the words of the clearing statement for it to work because it's about the energy.

Meaning of the ACCESS CONSCIOUSNESS CLEARING STATEMENT®:

www.theclearingstatement.com

EXPANDING OUT MEDITATION

CPSIA information can be obtained
at www.ICGtesting.com
Printed in the USA
LVHW040746100619
620692LV00002B/112